CHOICES AND DECISIONS

Drinking Alcohol

Pete Sanders and Steve Myers

Aladdin / Watts
London • Sydney

© Aladdin Books Ltd 2004

Designed and produced by
Aladdin Books Ltd
28 Percy Street
London W1T 2BZ

New edition
first published in
Great Britain in 2004 by
Franklin Watts
96 Leonard Street
London EC2A 4XD

ISBN 0 7496 5401 5

Original edition published as
What Do You Know About –
Drinking Alcohol

A catalogue record for this
book is available from the
British Library.

Printed in UAE

Editor
Katie Harker

Designer
Flick, Book Design & Graphics
Simon Morse

Illustrator
Mike Lacey

Picture Research
Brian Hunter Smart

CONTENTS

Introduction   3

Alcoholic drinks   4

Why do people drink alcohol?   7

Getting drunk   11

Alcohol and the body   15

Alcohol and behaviour   18

Effects on relationships   21

Attitudes towards alcohol   24

Sensible drinking   27

What can we do?   30

Useful addresses and websites   31

Index   32

How to use this book

The books in this series deal with issues that
may affect the lives of many young people.

- Each book can be read by a young person
alone, or together with an adult.

- Issues raised in the storyline are further
discussed in accompanying text.

- A list of practical ideas is given in the 'What
can we do?' section at the end of the book.

- Organisations and helplines are listed for
additional information and support.

INTRODUCTION

> " At the time, I thought that drinking with my friends would make me fit in and I'd feel like part of the gang. But after a while I realised that drinking wasn't going to be the answer. "

Drinking alcohol is part of many people's social lives. It is often associated with having a good time. However, alcohol is a drug. It can have a damaging effect on the body and can cause emotional and physical problems if it is not used in the right way. Today, more people are drinking alcohol than ever before.

This book will help you to understand the issues about alcohol – why people drink it, how it affects your health and the impact that alcohol can have on people's lives. Each chapter introduces a different aspect of the subject, illustrated by a continuing storyline. The characters in the story are involved in situations which affect many people in their everyday lives. After each episode, we stop and consider the issues raised, and open out the discussion. By the end of the book, you will understand more about alcohol and be able to make your own choices and decisions about the part that drinking plays in your own life.

I thought it would make me feel more confident but I just feel out of control.

That's what Dad said. When he and Mum argued he said terrible things. He didn't mean them, but it really upset Mum.

You need to get some help, Chris. Please talk to Mum and Dad.

ALCOHOLIC DRINKS

"Sometimes, when I go to a party, alcohol is the only drink offered to me. It's difficult to ask for a soft drink when you want to join in and be part of the crowd.

Alcohol has been drunk in different forms for many centuries. Today, drinking alcohol is accepted in most societies, and there is a wide range of alcoholic drinks available.

The scientific name for alcohol is ethanol. This is produced by sugar, water and yeast combining in a chemical process called 'fermentation'. Different types of alcoholic drinks contain varying amounts of alcohol. Beer contains less alcohol than wine and is made from fermented grains, such as corn and barley. Wine is made from fermented grapes or other fruits. Distilled spirits, like gin and whisky, are stronger. They are made by heating fermented grains or wine. Sherry and port are fortified wines – a mix of wine with some spirit. Other ingredients can change the colour or flavour of drinks. Some alcoholic drinks do not even taste of alcohol.

Alcohol is sometimes a symbol of hospitality and may be offered at meals or on special occasions, along with soft drinks.

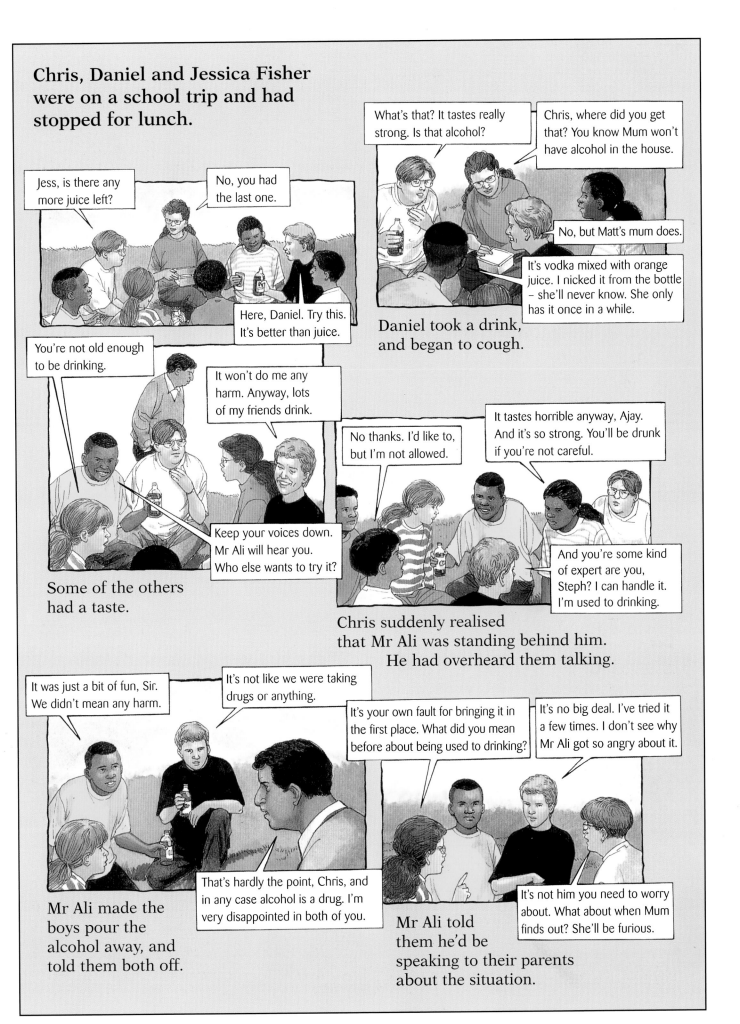

> It tastes horrible anyway, Ajay. And it's so strong. You'll be drunk if you're not careful.

Daniel and Steph know that some alcoholic drinks are much stronger than others.
Even drinks which look or taste similar can vary in their alcoholic content. The strength of alcohol is measured by calculating the percentage of ethanol in a drink. A small glass of wine and half a pint of beer equal one unit of alcohol. At home, drinks may not be poured to the exact measures used in pubs and restaurants so people may drink more than they realise.

> That's hardly the point, Chris, and in any case alcohol is a drug. I'm very disappointed in both of you.

Mr Ali said that alcohol is a powerful drug.
However, many people do not always view alcohol in the same way as other drugs. This may be because alcohol is legally and freely available to adults in most countries. But alcohol drunk in large amounts can have a serious effect on your physical and emotional health. Like drugs, people can become addicted to alcohol. This can affect many aspects of their personal life, such as relationships with other people. More people die each year from the effects of alcohol than from illegal drug abuse.

Alcohol and the law

● There are laws about the age at which people can buy alcohol in shops and drink alcohol in clubs or pubs.

● The consumption of alcohol is sometimes restricted in public places.

● There are laws about driving when under the influence of alcohol.

WHY DO PEOPLE DRINK ALCOHOL?

" I like to have a glass of wine when I get home in the evening. But then I have another and it seems a shame not to finish the bottle. "

People choose to drink alcohol for a variety of reasons. Many people enjoy the taste of alcohol and the immediate effects they experience having had a drink.

Some say that alcohol helps them to unwind and relax. People who are shy sometimes believe that alcohol will help them to overcome their fears. Many feel obliged to drink because of the social situation they are in. Some people drink out of habit.

Alcohol is often available in the most popular meeting places for adults – bars, pubs, restaurants and clubs. As a result, having a good time is often associated with alcohol being available. Because of this, it is easy for alcohol to become a regular part of a person's lifestyle.

Young people may begin to drink alcohol in order to impress others or perhaps because others dare them to do so. Drinking alcohol is often considered to be a grown-up thing to do.

Drinking is seen as an 'adult' thing to do. Advertisers are aware of this and often make drinking alcohol appear glamorous and sophisticated. This can often influence a person's decision to start drinking.

Today, some alcoholic drinks are also marketed towards the younger generation. Alcopops, for example, look and taste like soft drinks but contain relatively high levels of alcohol.

It was two weeks later...

... near the end of term.

Ali's so two-faced, going on about how drinking's bad for you. I passed the staff room and they're giving him a party later. And there was loads of booze in there.

I'm glad he's leaving this term. My dad never drinks alcohol so I got into real trouble because Ali told him about the school trip.

By the way, Josh Thompson invited me to a party at his house tonight. Do you want to come? It should be great.

I can't. Anyway, I didn't know you knew Josh. Since when have you been hanging around with him?

Not long. Josh's good fun. He's cool. He and his girlfriend look old enough to get into pubs and clubs. Come along tonight.

I'm in enough trouble. Mum and Dad grounded me for a month but at least they let me go to football practice.

Josh was two years ahead of them in school.

I thought Chris was coming too.

He was going to, but he changed his mind. He's gone out shopping with his friends.

He's hardly ever here these days. I hope he's not getting into any trouble.

Chris and Matt were both trying out for the school football team.

That evening, Daniel and Jessica went round to Steph's house. Their mothers worked for the same company, and the two families planned to go on holiday together.

I saw the doctor today. I'm going to have a baby!

Oh Chloe... James. That's wonderful news!

Congratulations!

Go on, Mum. Just a little bit.

Ok, just this once, as it's a special occasion. But just half a glass each.

Congratulations!

Congratulations!

This calls for a celebration. There's some champagne in the fridge. Let's toast the good news.

At dinner, Steph's sister Chloe and her husband James had a surprise for the family.

Mr Sharpe fetched the champagne. He asked if Daniel and Jessica could have some too.

... Steph, Daniel and Jessica went up to Steph's room.

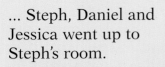

I can't believe Mum let us have a drink. She's usually so strict about it.

She's still upset about Dad, that's all.

Does he still drink?

Mr Fisher had begun to drink heavily after he lost his job and was unable to find new employment.

No, he seems fine now – at least he is on the weekends when we've seen him.

Before, he'd say that drink helped him forget his problems. But it just made him more unhappy.

Jessica said that her parents had begun to argue more and more.

Steph asked where Chris was.

They went on like that for months before they split up. Mum blamed Dad's drinking. She stopped having alcohol in the house. She was furious with Chris about the school trip.

He's at a party with Josh Thompson. Honestly, that's all he ever talks about now – how great his new friend is.

He's older, isn't he? I've heard the others talking about him – he's got a bad reputation. He's always in trouble.

Chris was late home that night. Daniel and Jessica heard him come in.

Where have you been? Mum's frantic. She's on the phone to Matt's house now, trying to find out where Josh lives.

So what? It was a great party. I couldn't care less what time it is. Tell Mum I've gone straight to bed.

But she'll want to talk to you. You can't expect us to cover for you, Chris.

She was all set to drive over to find you. What's the matter, anyway? You've been drinking, haven't you?

Chris refused to listen and went upstairs.

My dad never drinks alcohol so I got into real trouble because Ali told him about the school trip.

Some people, like Matt's dad, choose not to drink alcohol for a variety of reasons.

They may not like the taste of alcohol or they may know that it's bad for their health. Some people have religious or cultural beliefs which forbid the use of alcohol. Alcohol affects people's abilities and judgements. Lots of people choose not to drink in situations where they need to remain clear-headed. Sportspeople avoid alcohol because they know it will impair their performance.

Jessica and Daniel's dad drank alcohol to try to block out his unhappy feelings.

Some people drink as an escape from having to face up to situations they feel unable to handle. Alcohol may make a person forget their worries temporarily, but the problem remains when the effects of the alcohol have worn off. Using alcohol in this way can often make a situation worse.

Before, he'd say that drink helped him forget his problems. But it just made him more unhappy.

Peer group pressure to drink

When other people around you are drinking alcohol, you may feel pressured to drink.

- Some people make fun of others who do not drink.

- Drinking alcohol is a choice. You have the right not to do it.

- Drinking does not make you a better or more impressive person.

- The way that alcohol is presented in advertisements is often very different from the effect that alcohol can have in real life.

GETTING DRUNK

> I always know when I'm starting to get drunk.
> Alcohol usually makes me feel relaxed and
> carefree but sometimes, if I lose my inhibitions,
> I tend to make a fool of myself!

Even small amounts of alcohol can have a significant effect on your body and behaviour, whether you notice it or not.

Drunkenness is actually a form of poisoning. When somebody is 'drunk' they have consumed enough alcohol to severely affect their ability to function properly. The amount of alcohol it takes to get drunk differs for everyone. It depends on the age, sex, size and state of health of the person who is drinking. But even those who are similar in these respects may differ in their physical and emotional reactions to alcohol. The composition of women's bodies means that they tend to get drunk more quickly than men. Many people forget how easily drinking alcohol gets out of hand. Alcohol can alter moods and make some people argumentative or very sentimental. It can also affect a person's co-ordination, making walking and talking difficult. Alcohol also affects the ability to think clearly and to make rational decisions.

Being drunk is often seen as a bit of fun. Even people who know they have had enough will dare each other to have another drink. This can be dangerous, making you take risks you wouldn't otherwise take. If you get to know your limits it will help you to judge when you have had enough to drink.

... the Sharpes and Fishers went abroad on holiday.

> This is the life!

> Yes, if you like being bored to death.

> What is wrong with you? You've done nothing but moan since we arrived.

Chris said he was missing his friends and there was nothing to do in the hotel.

> There's a disco for us tonight. I'd like to go.

> That sounds like fun. I don't suppose you want to come with us to the cabaret?

> No way. I suppose a disco would be ok.

That night, Chris, Daniel and Jessica went to Steph's parents' room before the disco.

> You can't do that. My dad'll notice there's some missing!

> Don't worry. You can't have a disco without drink. Come on. Don't be such babies.

At the disco, Chris poured some whisky into Daniel's glass.

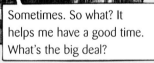

> It tastes strange. It's burning my throat.

> Do you drink this stuff a lot?

> Sometimes. So what? It helps me have a good time. What's the big deal?

An hour later, they were chatting to some people they had met.

> This is better than I thought it would be. How long are you here for?

> Another week. What's this?

> It's just wine. Justin got it on room service. He pretended to be his dad!

> We should go soon, Chris. I don't think Steph's feeling very well.

> Ok. The disco finishes soon, anyway. Let's go to the pool.

> Look at Justin and Nicole. They're dancing really close.

The four of them left soon afterwards.

Once outside...

... Chris started to fool around.

Chris, get down from there. That's dangerous.

I need to get back to the room. I think I'm going to be sick.

They sneaked into Steph's room, hoping her parents would be out.

Steph's not well. She must have eaten something dodgy.

Drunk something more like. Look at you. What have you been up to?

Sorry, Mr Sharpe. Some other kids had some drink with them. We thought it would be ok.

The adults came into the room. Mrs Sharpe went to look after Steph.

Are you sure they were the only ones with some alcohol? My whisky bottle seems rather empty.

I've warned you about this, Chris. You're taking after your dad. You're staying with me all day tomorrow.

We only took a bit. This has nothing to do with Dad. Anyhow, you're all drinking. I'm sick of everyone treating me like a child.

Chris stormed out. Mrs Sharpe came out of the bathroom.

Steph's fine. She's been really sick, but that's probably for the best. We obviously can't trust you on your own.

We're sorry about taking the whisky. We didn't mean it. It just got out of hand.

Chris is right. How come it's ok for you all to drink?

We're all adults, and we're responsible enough not to be rolling about drunk.

No-one said there was anything wrong with having a drink, Daniel.

I feel terrible. I'm not doing that again. How are you? Did you get into trouble?

Mrs Fisher sent Daniel and Jessica back to their room, and said she would be talking to them in the morning.

I thought I'd never hear the end of it. I don't feel too well, and Chris is being impossible. Mum's chatted to him but he just won't listen.

He walked out this morning, saying he was going to find Justin and Nicole. He's in a really strange mood.

13

I feel terrible. I'm not doing that again. How are you? Did you get into trouble?

Steph had a hangover the morning after she got drunk.

A hangover is the after-effect of the poison of alcohol on the body. It affects most people who drink a lot of alcohol. A hangover can cause headaches and feelings of nausea. It can also make people forget what happened when they were drunk and make it difficult for them to be fully alert for the whole of the day.

Look at Justin and Nicole. They're dancing really close.

Are Justin and Nicole moving too fast?
Many people find that they take risks when they are drunk. If the effects of alcohol cause you to lose your inhibitions, you may find yourself going along with a situation you would otherwise avoid. Accidents, fights, unprotected sex and criminal offences are all situations that may be fuelled by the consumption of alcohol.

Attitudes towards drunk people

People have very different attitudes towards people who are drunk.

- Some think that drinking a lot of alcohol is a sign of being masculine and is acceptable for men, but not women.

- Being drunk is not attractive, whatever your sex.

ALCOHOL AND THE BODY

> *When I woke up recently after a heavy night out, I felt terrible. My head hurt, I had no energy and I just wanted to stay in bed. It was such a waste of a day!*

Alcohol is absorbed into the body very quickly. Within minutes of having a drink, alcohol has reached the brain, muscles, nerves and other parts of the body.

Alcohol is a depressant drug. This means that it slows down the brain's responses, making reactions slow and muddling your thinking. As well as a loss of co-ordination, heavy drinking can cause vomiting and headaches. Long-term drinking can cause high blood pressure and serious damage to the liver, whose job it is to break down alcohol into less harmful substances. Alcohol can also harm the heart, brain and nervous system. If you drink a large amount of alcohol at one time, you are also in danger of slipping into a coma. Alcohol is very dangerous when taken with medications or other drugs.

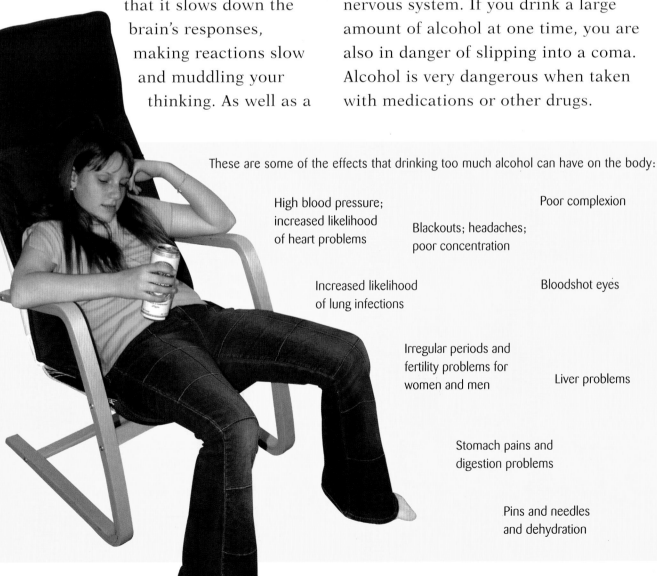

These are some of the effects that drinking too much alcohol can have on the body:

High blood pressure; increased likelihood of heart problems

Blackouts; headaches; poor concentration

Poor complexion

Increased likelihood of lung infections

Bloodshot eyes

Irregular periods and fertility problems for women and men

Liver problems

Stomach pains and digestion problems

Pins and needles and dehydration

On their return from holiday...

... the Sharpes took Chloe and James a present.

> Thank you. It's our favourite.

> We'll put it away until the baby's born though. I've decided not to drink alcohol while I'm pregnant.

> That's very sensible, darling. I think Steph could learn something from that kind of attitude!

Steph told Chloe about being drunk on holiday.

> It was Chris' idea, but it was my own fault for going along with him in the first place. I was a wreck for two days. It certainly wasn't how it looks on TV.

> She could hardly leave the room!

> Chris was really unfriendly towards us. He'd go off on his own or with Justin and Nicole. He was so moody. Daniel and Jess are really worried.

Two weeks later...

... Matt and Ajay ran into Chris in town.

> Hi, Chris. What are you up to? How was the holiday?

> Ok, I guess. I'm waiting for Josh. What are you two doing down here?

> We're on our way to the football pitches – where the two of us were supposed to go before you went on holiday. Remember?

> Yeah, sorry about that. I've been kind of busy. You know how it is.

> I hardly ever see you these days. But I see you've got some new friends.

> What's the matter with Chris? He looks a mess.

> Are you coming, Chris? I've got the stuff.

> He's really changed recently. We'd arranged all sorts of things for the holidays, but he just keeps making excuses.

Chris said he'd see Matt around, and left with Josh and his friends.

Matt was worried that Chris would get into trouble if he wasn't careful.

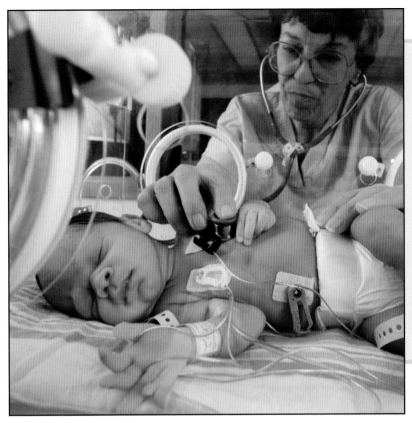

We'll put it away until the baby's born though. I've decided not to drink alcohol while I'm pregnant.

Chloe knows that alcohol can harm an unborn baby.
Alcohol in a mother's blood can pass to her growing baby. A baby born to a heavy drinker may have physical and mental abnormalities. Doctors advise pregnant women to be very careful about the amount of alcohol they drink.

He's really changed recently. We'd arranged all sorts of things, but he just keeps making excuses.

Matt knows that people can become physically dependent upon alcohol.
This means that their bodies become so used to the effect of alcohol that they seem to crave alcohol. They may wake up shaking, and the only way they can think of stopping this is by taking another drink. In this way, they become more and more addicted to alcohol, both physically and emotionally. If a person becomes addicted to alcohol it can seem to take over their whole life. Daily activities become centred around being able to have another drink. This can severely affect a person's motivation and their relationships with other people.

Alcohol and your appearance

Alcohol doesn't just affect the inside of the body. It can make a difference to your appearance as well.

- Alcoholic drinks have a large amount of calories which can lead to weight gain.

- Alcohol may make you look and feel run-down and cause you to have an unhealthy complexion.

ALCOHOL AND BEHAVIOUR

" I didn't think I was upset at the time, but after a few drinks I just couldn't stop crying. Last time when I was drinking I had fun, but this was totally different. "

Alcohol can significantly affect the way a person feels and behaves. A drunk person may not even realise that they are acting any differently.

Alcohol is an unpredictable drug. It can make people feel confident and in control, even though it is really clouding their abilities and judgement. People who have had a drink have a greater chance of having accidents, because they are unable to judge situations carefully. They may also be persuaded into situations which they later regret.

Behaviour may not always be consistent. Someone may be happy one moment, but angry or violent the next. The effect of alcohol on a person's emotions and behaviour often depends on how he or she was feeling beforehand. It can make people more depressed even though they may have drunk in order to feel good. But it can also make people miserable, even if they felt fine before drinking. Long-term alcohol abuse, or the effects of a hangover, may force people to take time off work.

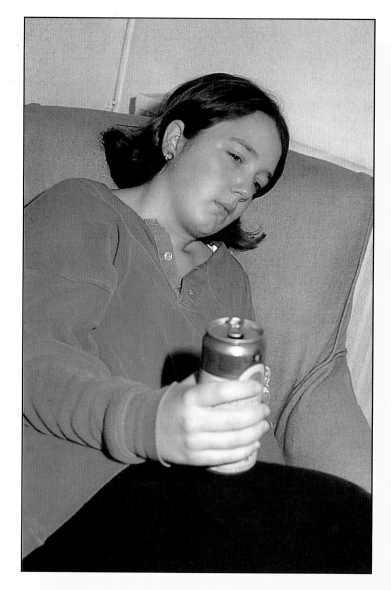

People cannot control the effect that alcohol has on their feelings. Sometimes, alcohol can make a person feel happy, but another time it may make them very tearful and emotional.

A few weeks later...

... Chris told his mum he was ill and couldn't go to school.

Steph caught up with Daniel and Jessica on the way to school.

> This is the third time since term started that you've missed a day. And I'm so used to the signs that I know you're drunk, not ill. Why won't you talk to me?

> I'm ok. Leave me alone. I just don't feel well, that's all.

> Mum told me your mum and dad might be getting back together. Is it true?

> We hope so. Nothing's certain yet, though. That's why we haven't really told anyone.

> It's great having Dad around again. They don't want to rush things, though. Dad got into quite a lot of debt with his drinking.

That evening...

> Mum keeps joking about how much all the taxis are costing them.

> I thought your Dad drove.

> He does, but he lost his licence last year for drink driving.

Mr Fisher had been banned from driving and had to pay a large fine.

... Matt met Chris in the street, with Josh Thompson. He could tell they had both been drinking.

> I went round to your house when you didn't come to school. Mr Dyton was asking about you. You missed football practice again.

> Who's this, Chris? He sounds like your mother.

> Who cares about football practice? I've got more important things to do.

> Like what? Getting legless? Oh yeah, that's very clever. You'll get into trouble if you go on like this.

> Get out of my way or you'll be sorry!

> Serves you right. I didn't ask for your opinion. I know what I'm doing.

> I thought we were mates, but you've changed so much.

Matt tried to reason with him. Suddenly, Chris lashed out with his fist.

Chris left with Josh. He was upset at having hit Matt. He had never done anything like that before.

19

Get out of my way or you'll be sorry!

Chris has been drinking, lost his temper and hit Matt.
Many people involved in violent incidents have been drinking alcohol. Alcohol lowers a person's self-control. Violence can be sparked off by a chance remark or for no apparent reason. Alcohol can also make people misjudge just how agressive they are being.

He does, but he lost his licence last year for drink driving.

Emotional dependence on alcohol

Drinking can become so much a part of a person's life that he or she feels unable to do without alcohol.

- People may rely on alcohol to help them to cope with all kinds of situations.

- They believe that if they stop drinking life won't be as much fun.

- If they began to drink to make themselves feel more confident, they may feel uncomfortable without an alcoholic drink.

- An emotional dependence on alcohol often means that a person is, or will become, physically addicted as well.

Mr Fisher put himself and other road users at serious risk by drink driving.
Every year, people are killed or badly injured by people driving whilst under the influence of alcohol. Many countries have strict laws about drink driving. Driving requires much skill and concentration, but drinking alcohol interferes with a driver's ability and judgement. Many people believe that drivers shouldn't drink alcohol at all.

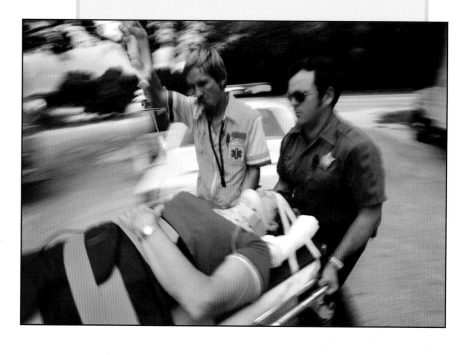

20

EFFECTS ON RELATIONSHIPS

It became impossible to connect with her once the drinking started. Our friendship was put under a real strain – it was only later that we were able to pick up the pieces again.

As well as damaging a person's health and well-being, alcohol can affect relationships with other people. Relationships can suffer as a result of even just a few drinks.

People who have had an alcoholic drink may say things they don't mean and small arguments can be blown out of proportion. Someone who gets drunk regularly may become unreliable because alcohol can affect a person's memory. People who are dependent on alcohol will think of little else other than drinking. They may try to hide the problem. If you live with someone like this, you may feel no longer able to trust the person. Some people grow to feel ashamed of a person they still love very much. More often than not, it is the people closest to a person with an addiction who are most affected.

Alcohol can make someone who is usually very quiet become suddenly violent. Or they may become unpredictable and neglect the people closest to them.

The next evening...

... after school, Chris' teacher Mr Rogers, asked him to stay behind.

I'm disappointed in your work, Chris. You're a bright boy, but you don't seem to care whether you do well or not. Is there something wrong?

No, everything's fine.

Well, something's the matter. You've been off school, your work's suffering and you've been missing football practice. Chris, you can always come to me if you need to talk.

Deep down, Chris did want to ask for help, but he was afraid to admit he had a problem.

The next morning...

... Daniel and Jessica came into Chris' room.

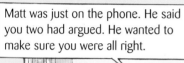

Matt was just on the phone. He said you two had argued. He wanted to make sure you were all right.

Did he tell you I'd hit him, too? I didn't mean to. I'd been drinking and I just flipped. I don't really understand what's happening.

Chris said Josh had thought the whole thing was just a joke.

He and his girlfriend get so aggressive when they've been drinking. It's not as if Josh's parents drink. It's frightening what drink can make you do. I've even been stealing from Mum to pay for it.

I thought it would make me feel more confident, but I just feel out of control.

They'll know what to do.

They're both worried about you.

That's what Dad said. When he and Mum argued he said terrible things. He didn't mean them, but it really upset Mum.

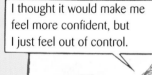

You need to get some help, Chris. Please talk to Mum and Dad.

Chris knew he needed to talk to someone.

Give me a bit of time to think. I feel like I've let them both down. You'd think I'd know better, especially because of Dad.

22

You're a bright boy, but you don't seem to care whether you do well or not. Is there something wrong?

Every person needs to feel a sense of their own worth.
A drinking problem can severely affect a person's sense of their own value. They may lose interest in themselves and those around them. It can be upsetting if you are treated badly because of someone else's problem. But remember, it's not your fault. If a situation is making you unhappy, it can help to talk to an adult whom you trust.

Young people may feel they have to cover up for the behaviour of parents who drink too much.
They may think there is nothing they can do about the problem and feel that they have to make excuses for the person concerned. They might also worry about what others will think if they find out. It can be hard to hear people saying unkind things about a person you love.

Unable to think clearly

People who are drunk are often unable to think and talk sensibly.

- People may start arguing when they are drunk.

- A drunk person may not make very much sense when they argue or be able to offer a logical argument.

- People who are drunk can sometimes become aggressive and very irrational.

- It can be upsetting if someone you love argues whenever they are drunk.

23

ATTITUDES TOWARDS ALCOHOL

> " It's difficult to admit to people that I don't drink alcohol. It's very rare not to drink and many people think that because I choose not to drink alcohol, I can't be much fun. "

In many societies, drinking alcohol is an acceptable choice. However, people have very different viewpoints on the subject. Many believe that because alcohol is so widely used and available, there is a danger of forgetting the problems that it can cause.

Those who try to make others aware of the risks, or who choose not to drink alcohol, are often seen as killjoys, because of the way people associate alcohol with a good time. Some organisations campaign for action to be taken against alcohol abuse and for stricter regulations regarding the consumption of alcohol, particularly in relation to drinking and driving, and to violence. Studies have shown that the risk of being injured or killed in a car crash increases directly with the level of alcohol a driver has consumed. Similarly, football hooliganism has often been related to excess alcohol consumption. Football grounds now restrict the levels of alcohol that can be taken to matches. Police surveillance at mass demonstrations also tries to limit the use of alcohol, to prevent violence.

Some drinks are advertised in a glamorous way. This contrasts with the actual effect that drinking them has on people. A person who has been drinking is rarely considered to be attractive to a sober person.

24

A few days later...

... Chris told his parents everything.

I liked doing it. It made me feel good at the time. I never thought it would get so out of hand, even though I knew what you'd gone through.

I know, Chris. I used to think of myself as a social drinker. It took me a long time to realise that the alcohol was controlling me and not the other way round.

The important thing is that you're talking to us.

I thought you were ok. But I should have known, you're just wet. Don't expect any favours from me.

Chris walked away, and went to find Matt.

You should have been like Ajay. He's not allowed to drink alcohol because of his religion.

But that doesn't mean I wouldn't like to, sometimes. Especially with the way they make it look in films and things.

Ajay said that lots of his Hindu friends drank alcohol, even though they weren't supposed to.

A couple of days later...

... after school, Josh Thompson came over to Chris.

Hey, Chris, where have you been hiding? Are you on for tonight? Bring some money, I'll get the drink in.

I'm sorry, Josh. I can't hang out with you any more. It's just not working out.

Don't worry, I won't. See you around.

I'm really sorry about what happened before. I was out of order.

You bet. Look, forget it. I'm just glad you're ok.

Chris told him he was doing much better. He'd even persuaded Mr Dyton to let him try out for the football team again.

I saw Josh Thompson last night. He and his mates were hanging out by the shopping mall, fooling around.

I'm glad Chris isn't part of that lot any more.

The next day...

... Daniel and Jessica were round at Steph's house.

25

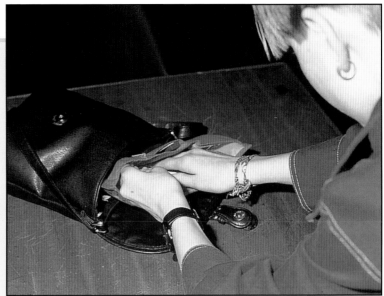

> Are you on for tonight? Bring some money, I'll get the drink in.

Chris knows that alcohol is expensive to buy.
People who are dependent on alcohol can run up huge debts, or even turn to stealing, to pay for their habit. Governments earn a lot of money from taxes on alcohol and businesses make millions from its manufacture. Alcohol is therefore likely to remain a legal drug in most societies for many years. It is important to know the effect that alcohol can have on your life if not used sensibly.

> He's not allowed to drink alcohol because of his religion.

Some cultures and religions do not allow the drinking of alcohol.
Even so, if you live in a society where alcohol is accepted and available, it can sometimes be difficult to refuse. It can cause great upset if a member of a family, whose culture forbids the drinking of alcohol, chooses to drink. As Ajay has said, the way in which alcohol is presented in the media can make it seem very tempting.

Social drinking

People in many social situations often drink alcohol automatically.

- They may describe themselves as a 'social drinker', intending this to mean that they do not have a problem with alcohol.

- Often, social drinkers do not realise the amount of alcohol they are consuming. They may actually be dependent on the alcohol without realising it.

SENSIBLE DRINKING

" I drink when I go out, but sometimes I just have one or two glasses of wine and then go on to soft drinks for the rest of the night. "

Alcohol need not become a problem if you understand the risks and develop a sensible attitude towards it. Many teenagers are naturally curious about what drinking alcohol is like. And most people will experiment and try alcohol when they are growing up.

Whilst one or two drinks are not likely to do any lasting damage, it's important to remember that young people can develop an addiction to alcohol just as easily as adults can. When you are growing up your body also undergoes many changes, especially during puberty. During this time it is not healthy to give your body the extra demand of breaking down alcohol. Every person has the right to decide to drink or not to drink. The decision will depend on lots of factors, including your age, experience and attitudes towards alcohol. It is important not to feel pressurised into drinking just because other people think you should. In the same way, if you do eventually decide to drink alcohol, you should respect other people's decisions not to, and not try to force them into doing something they don't want to do.

Alcohol plays a large part in many social occasions, but you always have the choice to say no to the offer of alcohol, at any time.

It was two months later...

... near to Christmas. The Fishers were having a small party.

Mr Fisher went to get some food.

Chris said he'd tried to talk to Josh, but Josh wouldn't listen.

The four of them went to join the others.

Anyone who feels that they have an alcohol problem should not be afraid to ask for help, at any stage.

Chris knows that talking about his feelings earlier would have helped prevent the problem from becoming so serious. Now, he has started going to a group. There are many counselling services and groups available all over the world. Many people with a serious problem will need to cut down on the amount they drink or give up alcohol altogether. This can be very difficult, but it can be done. People may need much encouragement from those close to them. There are many organisations which offer help and support to the family and friends of people who have a drinking problem.

I feel a lot better, thanks. I've also joined a local group that encourages you to talk about alcohol and stuff.

Oh, alcohol's ok. You just have to watch how much you drink. Come on, let's get something to eat.

If you drink alcohol you can take steps to avoid developing a problem.

Eating something during or before drinking will slow down the rate at which alcohol is absorbed. Different kinds or strengths of drink should never be mixed. It is a good idea to alternate between an alcoholic and non-alcoholic drink. Anyone arranging a party should make sure that there is a range of non-alcoholic drinks available. People should always feel free to refuse an alcoholic drink if they don't want one. Everyone who drinks alcohol should think carefully about the amount they consume.

WHAT CAN WE DO?

> It's nice to be able to have a drink now and again. But I don't have to rely on alcohol to have a good time.

Having read this book, you will understand more about alcohol and the effects it can have on people's lives.

Alcohol is a drug. Although it is legal in most countries, like all drugs it can do serious damage if it is not used properly. As you get older, you may be eager to try new things. But it's important to be aware of what experimenting might involve, and not to put yourself at risk. You know that alcohol does not make anybody more sophisticated or grown up. Drinking should be an enjoyable part of a person's social life. If you drink alcohol, look again at your reasons for doing so and consider the effect that alcohol might be having on you and those close to you. It's unlikely to be a problem, but it's always worth reassessing your relationship with alcohol. It's also never too late to seek help if you, or a friend, find that alcohol is getting the better of you.

Adults can help, too, by realising that their attitude towards alcohol can influence their children's views about drinking. If children see parents or relatives using alcohol freely, and perhaps getting drunk, they may come to view this as acceptable behaviour.

Children and adults who have read this book together may find it useful to share their thoughts and ideas about the issues raised. Information, advice and support can also be obtained from the organisations listed below.

Advice and Counselling on Alcohol and Drugs
14 Park Row
Bristol BS1 5LJ
Tel: 0117 929 3028
Email: info@acad.org.uk
Website: www.acad.org.uk

Alcohol Concern
Waterbridge House
32-36 Loman Street
London SE1 0EE
Tel: 020 7928 7377
Email: contact@
alcoholconcern.org.uk
Website: www.
alcoholconcern.org.uk

Alcoholics Anonymous
PO Box 1
Stonebow House
Stonebow
York YO1 2NH
Tel: 01904 644026
Helpline: 0845 769 7555
Email: newcomer@
aaservice.org.uk
Website: www.alcoholics-
anonymous.org.uk

Alcoholics Anonymous Family Groups
61 Great Dover Street
London SE1 4YS
Tel: 020 7403 0888
Email: alanonuk@aol.com
Website: www.al-anonuk.
org.uk

Adfam
(Families, drugs
and alcohol)
Waterbridge House
32-36 Loman Street
London SE1 0EH
Tel: 020 7928 8898
Email: admin@adfam.
org.uk
Website: www.adfam.
org.uk

Childline
45 Folgate Street
London E1 6GL
Tel: 020 7650 3200
24-hour helpline:
0800 11 11
Textphone: 0800 400 222
Website: www.
childline.org.uk

Drinkline
Weddel House
13-14 West Smithfield
London EC1A 9DH
Tel: 020 7332 0202
Helpline: 0345 320 202

Support for Children Affected by Drink (SCAD)
(Helpline for young people worried about someone with an alcohol problem)
10 Sansome Place
Worcester WR1 1UA
Tel: 01905 23060
Helpline: 0800 318272

Addaction
Central Office
67-69 Cowcross Street
London EC1M 6PU
Tel: 020 7251 5860
Email: info@addaction.
org.uk
Website: www.addaction.
org.uk

Youth Access
(Information, advice and counselling services for young people throughout the UK)
11 Newark Street
Leicester LE1 5SS
Tel: 0116 255 8763

Alcohol & Other Drugs Council of Australia
PO Box 269
Woden ACT 2606
Australia
Tel: 00 621 6281 0686
Email: adca@adca.org.au
Website: www.adca.org.au

Alcohol Drug Assocation New Zealand (ADA)
PO Box 13-496
First Floor
215 Gloucester St
Christchurch
New Zealand
Tel: (03) 379 8626
Email: ada@adanz.org.nz
Website: www.adanz.org.nz

INDEX

A

abilities, effect on 10, 11, 20

addiction 6, 17, 20, 21, 27

advertisements 7, 10, 24, 26

aggression 11, 18, 20, 21, 23, 24

alcohol, attitudes towards 14, 24

alcopops 7

appearance 15, 17

B

beer 4, 6

behaviour 11, 18, 21, 23

blood pressure 15

brain 15

C

choice and responsibility 10, 23, 27, 29

confidence, feelings of 7, 18, 20

counselling 29, 31

D

death 6

driving 20, 24

drugs 6, 15, 30

E

emotions, effects on 6, 10, 11, 18, 20

ethanol 4, 6

F

fermentation 4

H

hangover 14, 18

health 6, 10, 11, 14, 15, 17, 18, 20, 21, 26, 27, 29, 30

help, asking for 29, 30, 31

I

ingredients of drinks 4

L

law 6, 24, 26

liver 15

M

memory 21

men and women 11, 14

money and alcohol 26

muscles 15

N

nerves 15

P

parents' drinking 23

peer pressure 10, 27

pregnancy 14, 16, 17, 28

R

rationality 11, 14, 18

relationships, effects on 6, 21, 23, 30

religious and cultural beliefs 10, 26

S

safety 11, 14, 18

sex and alcohol 14

social drinking 7, 20, 24, 26, 27, 29, 30

soft drinks 4, 7, 29

spirits 4

strength of alcoholic drinks 4, 6, 29

U

unhappy feelings 10, 18

units of alcohol 6

W

wine 4, 6